T0288064

Visible Instruments

Visible Instruments

Michael Kelleher

chax
2017

Library of Congress Cataloging-in-Publication Data

Names: Kelleher, Michael, 1968- author.
Title: Visible instruments / Michael Kelleher.
Description: Victoria, TX : Chax Press, [2017]
Identifiers: LCCN 2016052320 | ISBN 9781946104069
   (softcover : acid-free paper)
Classification: LCC PS3611.E42 A6 2017 | DDC 811/.6--dc23
LC record available at https://lccn.loc.gov/2016052320

Author Acknowledgements
The author would like to thank the editors of the following
publications, in which several of these poems have appeared:
*ixnay reader, EOAGH, Glitter Pony, On Barcelona, The Colorado
Review*, and the anthology *A Celebration of Western New York
Poets.* He would also like to thank his mother for letting her use
her empty house to write in while she summered in her RV.

Publisher Acknowledgements
Chax Press would like to thank the University of Houston-
Victoria School of Arts & Sciences for its support and to
thank our press assistants for their hard work and good spirits,
namely Gabriela Delao, Sophia Kameitjo, Julieta Woleslagle,
Maria Edwards, and Renee Raven.

for Lori

CONTENTS

No music as accompaniment,
support or reinforcement.
No music at all!
(Except, of course, the music played
by visible instruments.)

— Robert Bresson
Notes on the Cinematographer

THE GOD POEM

For Rodolphe Gasché

That there might in fact be but one idea
In the whole history of human thought
Worthy of attention, and that that one
Idea can be expressed in a word and
That that word alone, that idea, is
The only one, despite or even because
Of its being a fabrication,
An untruth, a lie, both logically and
Scientifically indefensible,
Making it something akin to—yet
In duration, reach and depth exceeding—
That highest of the so-called human
Attainments, that is to say, Art, to which
We knowingly and willingly devote
So much of our attention, not to mention
Our money and time and intellectual
And spiritual energy, but which
Pales in the face of the concept of God,
A being or force or energy that
Transcends all time and space, giving birth
Ad infinitum to The New, able

To move forward or backwards in time,
For instance to the sudden explosion
That brought into being the universe,
Before even that, to whatever was
There to explode and to wherever 'there'
Actually was and if there was more
Than one 'there' there, that is, more than one
Universe expanding, an infinity
Of universes burning up and out
Whose infinite deaths leave infinite trails
Of past life in the form of particles
And/or waves of light that dance about
The heavens, refracted and reflected
Off an infinite number of floating,
Spinning, flying, careening things like moons
And stars, like asteroids and planets, some
Of which, like planet earth, have awakened
To these phenomena, and have chosen
To receive and collect, to analyze
And interpret their various meanings,
Have chosen to give these bountiful yet
Seemingly insignificant waves and/
Or particles of light a meaning, i.e.,
God, or the idea of God, which idea

Might be explained as human failure to
Comprehend the meaning of light and its
Attendant manifestations, which so
Often go unnoticed in the daily thrum
Of living, requiring us all to
Eat and sleep and drink and seek out the things
That will sate these needs, leaving little
If any time at all, even among
The diligent hordes of interpreters
Holding the various interpretive
Positions within the infinite
Number of disciplines invented
To aid the human race in its quest
To discover within the profusion of
Data received on any given day
A unified field of understanding,
One so comprehensive, so complete,
As to explain the whole universe of
Phenomena by means of a single equation,
Which function was preceded by the use,
From time immemorial, of a single word,
'God,' the subject of this poem, possibly
The single most beautiful false idea
And for so being the most worthy of our

Attention, and so the poem continues
And the idea of God endures in all
Its fruitfulness, as inspiration,
Guiding light, organizing principle,
Ideal, catch-all explanation, mysterious
Source of human power, moral bludgeon,
Ethical center, justification
For war and all imaginable kinds
Of craven human behavior, basis
For ideologies of every stripe,
Every one of whose precedence lies
In either the belief that God stands atop
A ladder and that human hierarchies
Are but natural imitations of same,
Or that we're all born equal in God's eyes,
And therefore justice (or property or
What-have-you) must be equally parceled out,
And where would any of these ideas
Have been without the idea of a God
Who both loves and punishes, all in
Equal measure, be it now or in the
"Hereafter," another beautiful idea,
In which every human consciousness
Lives on, intact and aware of itself,

Long past the death of the physical body,
This hereafter often being called "heaven,"
That place beyond death to which humans aspire,
And wouldn't that be nice, to know that
After death there is another life,
A better life than this, in which
Necessity is finally forgot,
Where no one wants and no one lacks and all
Are one and the same, and how this idea
Is nearly as lasting as the idea
Of God, if not quite so, how the idea
Of God endures despite all subsequent
Contradicting facts, despite the patent
Absurdity of believing in
An entity beyond all time and space,
Not only eternally fruitful, not just
The end and beginning and middle and
Purpose of all living things, but also
Sensitive to every being and object,
Every energy, every movement,
Every force and counterforce, every change
In weather or plans or disposition,
Responsive to each and every being
Across the broad expanse of its creation,

The absurdity of that, of all belief
And yet the utterly compelling beauty
It has inspired, the millennia
Of paintings, sculptures, poems, and musical
Compositions, the rituals, rites and
Dramas, the comedies and tragedies,
The sitcoms and miniseries,
The video games and epic films,
Not to mention the great books devoted
Solely to telling the story of God's
Eternal dance with human beings, how these
Books have at times inspired fanatical
Concentration on the meaning of the words
That were written therein, as if they were
Transcriptions of the words of God himself
Or herself or itself and so they came
To believe they could divine from these
Organized collections of signs not just
A meaning, eternal and fixed and true,
But an intention, that is, *the* intention
Of God, not only what God wants the words
To mean, but what God wants those who read
The words to do, how God wants them to behave,
To rein in their desires and by so doing

Achieve a kind of triumph over time
And space, wherein consciousness will live on,
Happy and free, in the aforementioned
Afterlife, and how these same books inspired
Other schools of interpretation that
Believed the words on the page could not have
Been written by God because the words them
-selves are imperfect, riddled as they are
With ambiguity and error, how
They refuse time and again to stand still,
Bearing within each one such a wide
Multiplicity of meanings it would
Take a literal eternity to
Interpret them all, not to mention the
Difficulty in trying to find
Within that multiplicity a single,
Unified and stable intention, fixed
And eternal, from which might be deduced
A rigid and transparent code of conduct,
Applicable to all people at all times
And in all places regardless of
Historical context, and still there are
Others who believe the infinite
Plasticity of meaning is itself

A true reflection of the fecundity
And multiplicity of God and so
Worship him or her or they or it as
A principle rather than a deity,
Per se, in short, "everything is everything,"
For were it even a desirable end,
Then unity of intent would be
In fact the case, which so clearly it is not,
And why, why, would a perfect being,
Perfect in every way, including its
Infinite multiplicitousness,
Create a world reflecting neither
Its form nor its intent, the short answer
Being it would not, therefore God's
Infinite perfection consists of the
Infinite multiplicity of her
Or his or its creations, a concept
Not to be confused with another school
Of thought that argues, yes, yes, the universe
Is multiple and infinite, meaning
Contextual and relative and
Historically specific; however,
God is an irreducible unity,
And the multiplicity of creation

Is in fact a form of retribution
Meted out to punish human beings
For their transgression, namely the desire
To know the world as God, that is, to know
The world in all its multiplicity,
For which sin they must learn to suffer
The pangs of birth and the fear of death
And they have written stories about how God
Has punished and punished and punished
Human beings, at times to set examples,
At others to test the faithful's faithfulness,
And in one strand of thought the story goes
That God will one day send to earth a savior
To rescue human beings from themselves
And he will arrive with fire in his eyes
And love in his heart to punish the wicked
And carry the faithful to heaven,
And one day a man of great charisma
Comes along who holds much sway in the hearts
And minds of many, encouraging them
To sacrifice their social status,
Family lives, material possessions,
In order to follow him, and many do,
And they become annoying and preachy

And eventually provoke the ire
Of the authorities, who put the man to death,
And it is written he rose from the grave
And came to speak to his disciples, which
Fact lead them to believe that it was he
That God had sent, which declaration split
This school into two schools, Old and New,
The Old believing that the messenger
Sent by God had yet to appear, the New
Believing he already had and shall
Return again to punish the wicked
And carry the faithful to heaven, how
This schism will alter human history
When the largest, most powerful empire
The world has ever known will consecrate
The New as official state religion,
And will rule the world for centuries hence,
Inspiring the construction of thousands
Of magnificent places of worship,
The majority built of stone, vast and
Mostly empty spaces, indirectly lit
By rays of sun refracted through panes
Made of colored glass illustrations of
Stories told in the holy book, literally

Illumining them for the faithful mass,
And these vast and mostly empty spaces
Would be owned and operated by
A worldwide community of celibate men
Who would throughout their history align
Their interests with the powerful, a long-
Lasting, mutually beneficial
Arrangement, but we're getting a bit
Off-topic, our topic being, you might recall,
That there is but one idea in history
Worthy of attention and that that idea
Can be summed up in a single word, 'God,'
All-seeing, all-knowing, all-feeling,
Infinitely creative, loving and just
In equal measure, rendering logical
Contradictions moot, how the history of
Ideas itself is but a history of
This one idea, the proverbial
"Elephant in the room," the elephant
With its great gray bulk and prodigious powers
Of memory being often a symbol of God,
Lurking at the margins of the argument,
Neither taking part nor taking sides,
Unsuspected, insistent and unseen.

VISIBLE INSTRUMENTS

The subject, you, sits writing at a desk.
Writing not in the sense of putting pen
To paper (here there is neither), but in
The sense of making meaning out of words.
Your fingers tap tap tap the letters on
A keypad, sending your computer an
Electronic signal, which sends it first
To a router, then to a modem then
Through a cable to a server to
Google Docs, which in turn sends it by
The same circuitous route as before
Back to your computer, where it makes
A digital letter on a screen. The
Process repeats until meaning is made.
This is known as "Cloud Computing." You
No longer sit writing at your desk, you
Transmit and receive signals from the clouds.
And then the rain begins to fall. It rains.

A sentence emerges: You will spend
The rest of your life in this place and will
Live each day in sequence, followed by

Another, and you will each day wonder
How in fact you ended where you are.
It is not the place you imagined you
Would choose to spend your life. Not this place.
A sentence emerges: a set of words
Complete in itself, which typically contains
A subject, You, a predicate, *will spend*,
Conveys a statement, question, command or
Exclamation consisting of a main
Clause, *You will spend the rest of your life*
In this place, and sometimes one or more
Subordinate clauses, a*nd will live each day*
In sequence, followed by another, and
You will each day wonder how in fact
You ended where you are. Etcetera.

You begin to list: a house, a car,
A job, a pet, a love. This is a form of
Reasoning, a making reasonable
Of something without reason. You begin
To list in the sense of leaning to one
Side, typically from a leak, or cargo
That's unbalanced. See *Heel*: to be tilted
Temporarily by the pressure of

The wind or by the inconsistent
Distribution of weight on board a ship.
You are listing now: a house, a car, a job, a
Pet, a love. Everything in balance, yet
'Desire' is another form of list:
As in, I have little list to write. Or,
As you might have said, this is an accounting,
Or better yet, a counting up. A one
And a two and a three and a four and
Five and six and seven eight nine. And ten.
A thing told is an account, the telling
Thereof an accounting. The subject, you,
Sits at a desk, making meaning out of words.
Or rather you send signals to the clouds
To make a list of things that give meaning to
Your life. A love, for example, a job,
A house, a pet, a car. Is there order
To this list? The thing that comes first to mind
Is thought to be the closest to the heart,
the heart that beats and beats and pumps the blood
that runs through veins into the brain, where one
is asked to share what comes to mind, assumed
To be the most important thing to you,
The subject. Thus is meaning made. And thus

The list that you, the subject, make, is telling.
Tell us what the lists you've made should tell us.

Why are you here? What are you doing here?
Why do you sit listing, making meaning
Out of words? Haven't you any better
Way to spend your time? Well, no, I don't. Wait,
Who said that? I said that. Who are you? I
I am 'you,' the subject of this sentence
That's emerging on the screen, the result
Of a series of rapid information
Transfers between a body at a desk
And a faraway cloud. It's part of a poem
Being written by you, the subject of
This sentence, who sits at a desk, making
Meaning out of words. The poem is the cloud,
Receiving and transmitting information.
It mixes signals often, sends them back
In different form. A sentence emerges:
You will spend the rest of your life in this place.
The sentence returns as a thunder clap.

Clap clap, clap clap, clap clap, clap clap, clap clap.
There's now no telling where the poem might go.

No longer clear who is writing, who is
Being written about, who is speaking,
Who is spoken to. You there, and you and
You and you. All are subject to the poem
And to the emergence of this sentence
Sentencing you to spend your life living
Each day in sequence, followed by another,
And to each day wonder how you ended
Where you are, and for which you, the writer,
Must account. Clap Clap Clap. This is the place
Where lightning strikes in the poem. Lightning strikes
A weeping willow tree. The tree begins
To burn. It heels in the wind. It lists. Tears
Won't help it now. The night is set ablaze.
Thousands of willows spontaneously
Combust. Clap clap clap clap. Clap clap clap clap.

SUNBATHER'S DIARY

It began when sitting by her husband's grave
The lovelorn lady sang. The city limits
Were crowded with donkey carts, yet
It's hardly clear that cars make people safe.
The weather is a refreshing seventy-two.
But what if all of this is just hot air?
(Note from *Hot Air Management*: this section
Is for comments_____). Measure the size, shape
And colour. Preserve a section, thinly sliced.
Make certain to begin with quality molds.
Not just any wax will do. No, I'm not kidding.
OMG…there are just no words. NO WORDS.
I may be statistically inconvenient
But I know I'm not unique. The madness
Doesn't stop. Malware is being upgraded
And then a deeper meaning appears
Regarding death and how you can't predict
The time or place. Pinging is currently
Not allowed. Question: Can I buy a star?
Answer: Who do you want to buy it for?
Hello. I am tired today. I am tired
This afternoon. I am tired this evening.

Hello there. I am bored tonight. I am a nice girl
Who would like to be chatting with you.
Did I dream that you dreamed about me?
Skip to the end to leave your response.
By late afternoon I'll be back in Bradenton.
My son and girlfriend are getting along,
Even though he's needy and controlling.
He tends to act and speak before he thinks.
His goal is to make slick-ass lover's funk
With no trace of irony. He can't repress
His need to entertain. His life at home
Is mellow with Dottie, his frigid wife.
Musing in bed I resolve henceforward
To rest upon my oars, to give up travel
By car. Ulysses is dead and shall
Never return to the land of the living.
What will my life in my sorrows be?
Attacked by bunnies in a dream last night,
He fell in the dust. And Achilles said:
Dogs and birds shall tear your flesh unburied.
Looking into my sad, droopy eyes, I
Recalled the smiling lessons I had bought
To keep at bay my face's wrinkled brow,
And then I said aloud, "Next subject, please."

I once dated an English girl. She said
She was born in a northern mining town.
She once came home with a cheap, no-name
Acoustic guitar. She'd been out all night.
I didn't ask her where she'd been because
I didn't want to know. I didn't care.
Her radiance never dims. She lived the rest
Of her days in the high solitude
Of the rare bird. I have been through a lot
And I do not feel like sharing anymore.
I recently was told the treatment
Isn't working. Suggestions, anyone?
In the sensual half-light of the club
One finds quiescence and devotion. Seeds
Of love are sown. High time we made a stand
And shook up the views of the common man.
Do you like girls with button noses?
Every time I see myself in the mirror
I always hate my button nose. I like
Long noses, antique watches, luxury cars
And beautiful homes. Many of us
Who love to decorate wonder at
The graceful curves and flowing form
Of the Japanese Maiko, a shining leaf

Floating down her obi, here and there
A parasol. Lord, let the skies weep tonight!
Please review these songs and tell me if they
Meet your needs. I'm in Florida. Feel free
To hit me up or just to say hello.
Hello out there. Are you truly happy?
I need to know and I need you to know
I have a problem I can't handle now:
I really like pizza, but it makes me sick.

THE LIBRARIAN

Circling around the island again and
Again. This should be filed under 'Sappho.'
It was one of those places I'm not sure
Existed. I can picture it upstairs
In the bookcase at our last house. Later,
We sat in my car, gossipping. He seemed
To have come out of the womb performing these
Grown-up tasks. I remember everything
Perfectly. My mind drifted as my eyes
Scanned the titles on the theory shelf. This
Went on for several years. A lover (man),
His love interest (woman), her pet sparrow.
Having cut my teeth on the difficult,
I put it in my pocket and walked out.
I stole lines, ideas, images, rhythms,
A voiceless glottal positive. Lifted,
Reshaped. An overwhelming feeling of
Heartbreak. Prose is too noisy a medium.
I want the writer to do something more
Than simply hold the mirror up. I want
Her to go way out. Then he saw and then
I saw and he said something like, Oh lord.

The struggles of the martyrs, yawn, these words
Are secretly dedicated to them.
And here's the famous windmill scene, Dear Heart.
I hope to sleep tonight and then begin
A mythopoetic excavation
In the morning. I want to dig it up.
It befalls us to wonder on this first
Astonishment. I have so many thoughts,
Most of them idle. I have a feeling
This is a gift, but I can't remember
Who might have given it to me. We spoke
Of how we'd often been in the same place
Without ever having met. He had been using
An oxygen tank. I never thought him
A tarot card kind of guy. We painted
And sang and danced and listened to stories.
The rest, as they say, is history, of
Which I can only read so much before
My eyes get bleary. The luxuriant
Beauty of the orange garden bears witness
To antiquity. He felt compelled to
Address it every time. Eventually
I discovered I preferred writing to
Generating text, an on-again-off

-again friendship, never quite requited.
I am standing before a wall of words.
My hair is pulled back in a ponytail
And I am wearing gold. How awed I feel.
I couldn't write another phrase. And then
The feeling of having been sitting through
An apocalypse. Three times begun and thrice
Have I failed. I don't think it is a sign
I'm losing steam, having as it does the feel
Of a thing very much still in process.
We stopped at a seafood shack by the road.
We played poker and yammered all night long.
I never could concentrate on my work.
I found him in his chair. He listened slowly
And closely. I thought of the woman on
The cover of the book of film theory,
Standing near the expressionistic door.
Someone somewhere shouted out my name.
An endless progression spiraling back
Into the genetic past. The empty
Marketplace, the weeds rising like fireworks
Through the floor, the character of a man
Divined by reading the shape of his hands,
Community gardens, luxury homes,

A former factory complex, the word
'Quonset,' the absence of time, the frantic
Planting of vegetables, the hitting of
The road, the one we always seem to hit,
The memory of old books behind glass doors,
Protected from the dust, or most of it,
The dog, its ears, the faint sound of riffling.

POEM IN A REAR VIEW MIRROR

I'm dreaming of urban renewal right now:
Entropy, abandoned homes, insurance
Scams, the Bronx is burning. When I recall
The past I'm actually in the past. My mind
Is blank. And then it was December. We
Were visiting my mother at Christmas.
I had nothing to read. Time, etc.
I had plenty to write about in my
Black marbled notebook. It was a nice day.
I wanted to go back to see if there was
Something there for me still. I didn't find
What I was looking for. I bought a book
To learn the alphabet. For instance: 'A'
Is for 'Agamemnon.' I find myself
Wishing for retribution. On a bench
In Central Park, the old guard seems to be
Getting phased out, and I am now too sleepy
To type out the fragments. The story opens
In a frigid field, the limits of which
Signal a beginning or an end. A young
Lover talking to himself about love.
They have a word for that. Anyhow,

My markings seem to indicate that I
Have read this passage before. Can you tell
I was educated by Jesuits?
Wild profusions of scrawl take over the page.
Beginning at the outer edge, at just
The point at which it rubs against the world,
The yellowing works its way inward, forming
An aura around the words, which will themselves
Succumb to this ineluctable dis-
coloration. One day the edges will crack
And the pages will biodegrade. The book
Will be no more. *O Rose, thou art Sick.*
Once I tried to write a poem by writing
The opposite meaning of every line
From another poem. It didn't really work.
At the time I had almost no money
And borrowed all of my books. Our first night
We ate dinner at a little bistro.
Seven feet of snow fell on the city.
It very nearly drowned her quiet voice.
I sometimes wonder if I I've actually done
The things I think I've done, known the people
I think I've known, lived in the places
I think I've lived, or if I've made it up

In order to please myself (and others).
We were living in our last house, the one
We sold that year, if memory serves, sitting
Outside on the porch, watching the children
Attack each other with chestnuts, so it
Must have been in early fall. We talked
About the various cities in which
We'd lived: New York, Vienna, Buffalo
Silverthorne, Washington, Los Angeles,
Quito, and the minor vicissitudes
Of living in the desert among an
Unfamiliar set of desert creatures.
The outcome, of course, was foretold.
The light from the lamp and the light from the flash
Canceled one another out. I let
The camera wander down to her hands, which
Gestured in ways that seemed to contradict
The things she said. There is, in essence,
No past. What we call 'past' is still extant,
Lost among the amassing details of time.
I was catching a nap in the lounge when
I was awakened by a rumbling.
In the center of the room, on top of
The desk, there sat a box of candy squares.

I chose a chocolate wrapped in golden foil,
And I ate it, and it was delicious.
I savored each bite; but then I thought
I should not have eaten that one. It was
The only one, and now it's gone. Indeed,
The ephemerality of thought serves
Often as a kind of double for the
Ephemerality of life. Now I'm
Feeling sort of sad, as if I could repent
Of something I have or have yet to do.

BUT DO THEY SUFFER?

I hadn't asked myself this question yet,
But then I read that essay, the one where
The late David Foster Wallace describes
In objective detail his moral qualms
About boiling lobsters, not of eating meat,
Crustaceans, or poultry, *per se*,
Just the specifics of boiling alive
A living creature that, it has been said,
Feels nothing, and where either sense of "feels"
Can be assumed, that is, it feels no pain,
Either emotional or physical,
Once it's been dropped in the pot, it just boils,
Or rather slowly becomes something else,
A light, fluffy, delicate entree served
With melted butter in a dipping cup,
So delicious, I remember my first
Time eating lobster as a boy, we sat
In a fire hall in a place called Freedom,
New Hampshire, it was summer, our family
Of five plus our cousins from Brooklyn
Escaping city swelter, my uncle
Brought a cassette tape with the soundtrack to

Star Wars, or so he said, but it was fake,
Not the real deal, they used synthesizers,
My father scolded me for saying so,
I remember crying after the slap,
Standing alone at the edge of the woods,
Staring into the darkness, wishing I
Or he were dead, I mean, like, what the fuck,
It wasn't the music we'd heard in the film,
My favorite film, BTW, whose
Release was to that point the most exciting
Event of my short, uneventful life,
I mean, it's Luke Freaking Skywalker, Dad,
Don't you get it? either it's the real thing
Or it's some shabby imitation, like
This synthesized falsehood calling itself
Music, a reminder also that life
Might be itself an imitation of
A perfect order that's forever out
Of reach, like in that quote from Kafka,
Further proof (to me, at least) that his sense
Of the real can be trusted, like the taste
Of lobster, to bring pleasure, but also
A sense there might be something else beneath
The surface of what we're consuming,

As sweet as it tastes, as soft as it feels
As it melts on the tongue going down,
Like that first time in Freedom, I recall
That while we ate we listened to a man
Tell jokes, he looked a bit like Milton Berle,
His jokes were vaguely racist imitations
Of Chinese proverbs, told with fake Chinese
Accent, front teeth Mickey-Rooneyed over
Lower lip, "Confucius say, he who eat
jelly bean fart in living color," or
"He who fart in church sit in his own pew,"
We laughed as we dipped our fresh Maine lobsters
In the butter sauce, God did they taste good,
It was as if I'd been eating the
Synthesizer-equivalent of food
My entire life, the flavor, the texture,
Everything about it, though I've eaten
Lobster many times since then, it hasn't
Ever tasted quite so good, as if I
Can recognize a few scattered fragments
Of the lobster in my memory, but
I can't find a way to bring it to life
In all its fullness (Kafka again), like
When I read as a child that my idea

Of God, which I'd learned about from my mom,
Was actually a memory, carried
Over from a previous life, which left
In its wake an idea of perfection
To which I should aspire, and of course fail,
Leaving in pieces my perfect idea,
Which I've tried to put together, and failed,
Producing at best a cubist image,
As in the "Nude Descending a Staircase,"
Like how once you're told the title you see
The staircase, the descent, perhaps the nude,
But you always wonder whether or not
Duchamp is really just messing with your head,
Leading you away from the truth, the real,
And you crane your neck around to catch it,
And all you see is the flicker of shadows
Dancing across the walls of your cave,
They're beautiful, don't you think? I could stare
At them forever, forgetting that they,
Too, are imitations thrown up by fire
To distract me, and why the hell not?
This is what struck me about that question
In the title of the poem, which comes from
Richard Dawkins, the famous atheist,

Who posed it not to meat eaters, but to
Those whose philosophical systems
Place *homo sapiens* at the center
Of creation, thereby relegating
Animals to their second-class status,
Allowing for cruel, senseless practices
Such as branding, castration without
Anaesthetic, and bullfighting which, he says,
We would never inflict on human beings
(Most of us anyhow), because we know
They would suffer physically, nevertheless
We allow such to occur, assuming
Either that animals do not suffer
Or that their suffering is not like ours, is
Of a lesser kind, cannot be perceived
Outside itself, therefore, for example,
As David Foster Wallace stated, we
Boil the lobster alive because we think
It doesn't feel, but evidence does exist
That seems to prove the contrary true, that
Banging its claws against the pot is not
An involuntary response, but can
And should be read as an expression of
Pain, as in, Ouch, that shit is hot, stop it,

Stop it stop it stop it stop it it hurts,
But if we felt like that we'd all go mad
With guilt over our own barbarity,
We might even follow the path of Foster
Wallace and have done with thinking for good,
Tie a rope to a transom and end it,
Just like that, leaving a pile of finished
Books and unfinished manuscripts behind,
The Pale King, I think it was called, did I
Tell you I met David Foster Wallace?
I drove him around town, took him to lunch,
We talked about Aristotle, he said
He thought I looked like actor Greg Kinnear,
I went home and looked on the Internet
For a photo and when I found one stared
Until I thought I could see a resemblance.

INTERIOR DESIGN STUDY

for Suzanne Stein

A table set with crackers, brie and grapes.
Four green mats, three wood chairs, an empty mirror.
I wonder what the mirror is doing there?
Reflecting, probably. Wrong to call it
'Empty.' Its circle leans against the wall.
The room is empty. That is what I mean.
The room is emptied of people; therefore,
The mirror too is empty. It reflects things
Nonetheless, at such and such an angle
(Because of the lean): four clear drinking glasses,
Of varied size but similar shape,
Empty, like the mirror, though their reflection
(Because of the angle) makes them look full,
Also the wooden frame of the window,
And through the window the reflected leaves
Of some overexposed vegetation.
Chairs pulled slightly at an angle out from
The table suggest, perhaps, a gathering.
Green grapes sit in a large, white bowl, the lip
Of which is flared, not flat, like the small one,
Also white, that holds the crackers. The brie,

A white wheel, softens beside a knife.
The tabletop is made of a dark wood.
The frame is metal. It looks to have been
Built directly into the plaster wall
On which hang three white sheets of paper,
Two of them notebook-sized. One window's closed,
Or rather covered by a pulled-down shade.
Two large, black binder clips grip its sides.
Two more binder clips cling to a hanging
Sheet of paper, the largest of the three,
As if to weigh it down. The bottom half
Is blank, the upper half is filled with text
Neatly arranged in columns, like stanzas.
The knife, the brie, the small white bowl hover
Atop a wooden cutting board resting
On the crease between two woven green mats—
Green and brown and maybe white, a fuzzy fringe,
Also green, and not a one reflected
(Because of the angle) in the mirror.
The floor is made of wood. A heater or
Air-conditioner fits under the sill,
The one over which we can see through glass
To the green leaves of the trees outside.
They, too, are overexposed. In the mirror

One can see something I-don't-know-what
Reflected. They're curled iron stems, I think,
A decorative element absent the field
Of vision proper. I want to sit down,
To eat the brie, the crackers, the grapes,
To fill those glasses with water, but who
Will be my company? Where will they sit?
Who will take the only metal chair?
Will they be comfortable? Should I take it?
You know, to seem polite. The mind wanders–
Away from what will no doubt be clever
Conversation–to the mirror, which, from the chair
One has taken, the metal one, reflects
The window, the frame, the shade, the trees, the sun.
This must be California. It's too bright!
The mind is suddenly dazzled. Outside
Is nature of a sort, sticky and hot,
Its constant vying, its bugs and beetles
And bears, like the one I saw in the dream.
It watched me from behind a low, wide tree
On an otherwise empty hillside,
And I was afraid because I'd been told
The worst thing to do if you see a bear
Is run, that you should make yourself seem huge,

Shout loud sounds to scare it off, but now
I could only feel my fear, fear of death,
More than that the fear of physical pain.
I was starting to run, but then the bear,
From its place behind the tree, smelled my fear
And it, too, began to run. I thought,
Stop, face it, make yourself huge, shout loud sounds,
But all I could do was shrink in my tracks
And wait for the bear to attack. It did,
And I awoke in a sweat before its claw
Could knock me down. About now I wonder
Where the guests have gone. Is there anyone
Here but me? Am I here? Or did I flee
The scene, having left the mirror at rest
Against the plaster of the cream-colored wall?

FREUDIAN POEM

File, open, document, enter, *voilà:*
The empty page. To fill it in with words
Expressing deep and powerful feelings
Like love and longing and loneliness and
Let it not be said we don't express
Those feelings here. Or rather let it be
Or seem to be as if we do. Feelings
After all are physical, think 'pang,' think
'Blush,' think 'chill,' or better yet, *'frisson.'*
(French cognates elevate English feelings.)
For instance when I feel a 'chill' I want
To wrap myself up in a blanket, but when
I feel a *frisson*, I want to make love.
When I left the page just then (an event
Of which no doubt you were until now
Unaware) I made a move in Scrabble.
'Skee' was the word I put down, like 'skeeball.'
Not 'put down' in the sense of 'suppressed'
Or in that other, meaning 'euthanize,'
As one might a cat or dog or hobbled horse,
But to 'put' the letters of the word 'skee'
'Down' on the Scrabble board. Not literally

'Down,' as I moved on a virtual board,
A 'screen,' if truth be told, though not quite that—
It was a 'monitor.' Thus, the phrase
Is not 'put down,' it is 'moved into place,'
A kind of lateral virtual slide.
One might reasonably inquire where
Or when these deep and powerful feelings
Will finally appear in the poem, to which
One might reasonably respond, 'They already have!
You missed it! Didn't you feel the *frisson*
When you read the word '*frisson*?' I suppose
You did not. The rule of thumb for poetry
Is to show and not tell. Feelings must be
Presented obliquely and not simply named.
How can one feel a word? One feels feelings
A word or phrase expresses. One does not
Feel them by speaking the words themselves.
Try this experiment: the following
Is a list of words describing feelings.
Speak each word aloud and when you do
Try to feel the feeling or emotion that's
Expressed: disgust, contempt, anxiety,
Loneliness, wonderment, happiness, awe,
Nostalgia, shame, lust, guilt, anger (I'm told

Anger is a secondary feeling
Masking other, more vulnerable feelings,
But here it is nonetheless), hatred, love,
Malice, sadness, anticipation, joy,
Trust, fear, surprise, disappointment, remorse,
Aggression, anticipation plus joy,
Joy plus trust, trust plus fear (I guess I forgot
To mention fear), fear, fear plus surprise, then
Surprise plus sadness, sadness plus disgust,
Disgust plus anger, anger plus anti-
Cipation, affection, zest, contentment,
Pride, enthrallment, irritation, relief,
Exasperation, rage, envy, torment,
Suffering, neglect, sympathy, empathy,
Horror, nervousness, adoration, zeal,
Fondness, liking, caring, compassion, bliss.
I got this list from Wikipedia.
It contradicts my claim that anger is
A secondary feeling, which idea
Came from my therapist. Now I wonder
Who I should trust, Wikipedia
Or my therapist. In the wiki-scheme
Of emotions I should now be feeling
The opposite of trust, that is, disgust.

But is disgust really trust's opposite?
I guess I'll leave that to professionals.
I do not feel disgust right now. I trust
No one. I never told my therapist.
She may or may not have intuited this.
Now I'm thinking of a line from a poem
By Ben Friedlander that says something like,
'I once stuck a carrot up my ass and
Lied about it to my therapist.'
I never stuck a carrot up my ass,
But have many times put my finger in.
I have never told my therapist.
I haven't told her, but I haven't lied.
One doesn't need to lie unless one feels
Ashamed. Sticking your finger up your ass
Is okay. No need to lie about it.
Not to anyone. Just stick it up there.
Go ahead. Try it. You probably did
It a lot when you were a kid until
One day your mother caught you and spanked you
And told you to stop. At that point you felt
Shame. You may be feeling shame again now.
That's ok. It's not really shame. It's your
Mother telling you to go wash your hands.

SHAGGY DOG POEM

I am told I can tell a good story.
My girlfriend, Lori, tells me I should write
My stories down and turn them into books.
By books she means 'novels.' By 'novels' she means
It might be nice if I got paid for writing.
It might be nice if I got paid for writing,
But I'm no novelist. My little voice
That tells me what to say tells me I'm
A storyteller who it happens writes poems.
The voice says that makes me a bad poet,
To which I often reply, It makes me
A narrative poet, to which the voice
Returns, You don't write narrative poems!
A gross oversimplification, I say.
But then I get to thinking I should write
A narrative poem. Just tell a story,
Cut it into lines and call it a poem.
(I think there's ample precedent for this.)
For instance, when I was a lad I heard
A story about a young boy, my age,
That is, about nine years old, who was told
By his friend at school to ask the teacher

The meaning of a particular phrase.
Ask the teacher what 'purple passion' means,
Said his friend. His teacher had told them that
The only bad question was the one that
Was never asked, so the boy raised his hand.
What does 'purple passion' mean? The teacher
Turned white, then purple, then green, and then red.
Very red. Come to the front of the class!
The little boy stood and walked to the front.
Repeat what you said. 'Purple passion.'
The teacher slapped the boy across the face.
I should here note that this story took place
Either in a Catholic school where such things
Still occurred when I was nine, or sometime
Before I was born, in the fifties perhaps,
When corporal punishment was the norm.
I have generally assumed, on the basis
Of my own experience in Catholic schools
That the former was the case, but one could
Make an argument for the latter.
For instance, the word 'purple,' circa
The fifties had different connotations
Than it does today, cf. the phrase
'Purple prose,' meaning extravagant,

Ornate or flowery writing that breaks
The flow of the narrative by calling
Attention to itself. The phrase derives
From a passage in the poet Horace:
'Your opening shows great promise, and yet
Flashy purple patches, as when describing
A sacred grove, or Diana's altar,
Or a stream meandering through fields, or
The river Rhine, or a rainbow. But this
Was not the place for them. If you could
Faithfully render a cypress, would you
Include one when commissioned to paint
A sailor in the midst of a shipwreck?'
One could quibble with Horace's question,
Especially given all we've come to know
About representation, mimesis,
Etcetera, in modern times. Why
Couldn't we paint a cypress in the midst
Of a scene of a sailor and a shipwreck?
Depending on the location of the wreck,
Its nearness to shore, and the local flora,
There might very well be a reason to
Place a cypress in the picture, and why not?
Why not paint it on the sailor's head or

Floating in the sky above the ship?
One would think an artist such as Horace
Would have already thought through these ideas.
At heart it seems he was a pedant,
Or maybe just a manly stoic, taut
Jaw, stiff upper lip, no patience for games
Of any kind. Just the facts, ma'am — that sort.
He would have fit right into the fifties
In America, ashamed and afraid
Of all things purple, especially passion.
After the teacher slapped the little boy
She sent him to the office, and bid him
Ask the principal what 'purple passion' meant.
He looked at his pal, who sat in back,
Smiling broadly, proud of the damage
He had wrought upon his erstwhile friend,
And wondered why this had happened to him.
I should also note that 'purple prose'
Can mean 'sensually evocative
Beyond the requirements of the text,' which
Could explain some part of the shock it caused
The little boy's teacher, which to be frank
Was nothing compared to the shock it gave
The principal when the little boy

Repeated it to him. He told the boy
To drop his drawers and spanked him on the ass.
He spanked and spanked until his ass burned red.
He sent him home and told him not to return.
The punishment was harsh but that's the way
They did it in the fifties, swift & severe.
What puzzled the little boy was that no
Adult would tell him what 'purple passion'
Meant. He trudged across the playground, over
A path through the woods that led to his house.
The house was a split-level ranch that sat
Atop a hillock on a *cul de sac*.
It had a steep driveway and a lawn,
A basketball hoop in front and a pool
In the back. His mother was a housewife,
As were many women back in the day.
His father was a businessman who worked
His way from the bottom to the middle
Selling things like vacuum cleaners and cars.
He was, like Horace, stern, pedantic, and
Demanding. Little patience had the man
For flowery words, much less forbidden ones.
When he got mad his face got very red,
Like the teacher's face, only redder, and

When he spanked he spanked harder and longer
Than the principal. He hoped that he might find
A sympathetic ear and told his mom
What he had said. But little did he know
That his father was in the other room.
He heard the forbidden words and shouted,
Where did you hear that phrase? At school, he cried,
But no one will tell me what it means!
I asked the teacher and the principal
And now they've sent me home to you. Oh, Dad,
What does 'purple passion' mean? His father
Turned red and screamed at the little boy.
You have shamed this house. You are not my son.
Go, and never return. I know this sounds
Over the top, but it's a true story.
It happened in the fifties, when fathers
Had more authority than they do now.
You see, in the sixties authority broke down.
Children stopped respecting their parents,
Their teachers, their principals, their priests
And their government. They started using
Words long forbidden in everyday speech.
This caused a great rift between old and young,
It was known as the ' Generation Gap.'

The gap was filled with rock 'n' roll and drugs,
But the gap was deep, a kind of chasm
That never could be filled, and never would:
And from this chasm, with ceaseless turmoil seething,
As if this earth in fast thick pants were breathing,
A mighty fountain momently was forced.
I didn't write that passage, it came from
Samuel Taylor Coleridge, only he
Wasn't writing about the sixties or
About the Generation Gap. Still, he
Could have been writing about these things,
If you think about it. Think about it.
Okay, that's enough. Samuel Coleridge
Himself was a user of drugs, although
This should not pollute our reading of
His poem, which, though hallucinatory,
Is a lucid fantasy of the first rank.
Nonetheless it could be argued that the
Poem's 'mighty fountain' represents
A breakdown of authority much like
America's in the sixties. Alas,
Out little boy's age was still paternal
And he was cast out, east of suburbia,
And so he wandered many years, a kind

Of wandering (Catholic) Jew, a pilgrim
Consumed with his desire to know just what
'Purple passion' meant. He asked the priests,
They threw him out of the church. When he asked
The police, they threw him in the slammer.
The charges didn't stick, for now it was
The sixties and phrases like 'purple passion'
Didn't carry the same taboo, thanks to
Allen Ginsberg and Lenny Bruce, but still
He could not find a person anywhere
Who would relieve him of his ignorance.
He grew to be a man, then an old man.
He lived on social security checks
And drank from morn till night. 'Purple passion'
Dragged across the blackboard of his soul like
So many fingernails. He went to see
A fortune teller. She opened his hand
To read the crooked creases in his palm.
You have suffered greatly. I have suffered.
You're life is incomplete. It's incomplete.
You're seeking the answer to a question.
I'm seeking the answer to a question.
There is only one who can answer this
Question, and that one lives far away.

I'll travel any distance. You must go
High into the Himalayas, find there
A sherpa to guide you to the temple,
And when you arrive at the peak, give thanks.
Make an offering to the mountain god.
Fast forty days and forty nights before
You ask the god to give you an answer.
I shall, and thank you dearly, said the man.
He stepped from the palm reader's parlor
To the sidewalk and the bright light of day.
He placed a hand above his eyes to read
The crossing sign before he crossed the street.
He stepped down into the crosswalk, but he
Failed to see a bus and got run over.
The moral of this story as it's told
Most often is that you should look both ways
Before you cross the street, but I'm not sure
The best lesson one can learn from this is
Quite so mundane. My little voice tells me
I've gone on too long. Just get to the point,
It says, by 'point' the voice means 'moral.'
Not that I want to quibble over words,
Except to say that 'point' suggests an end,
A terminus, a final destination,

A kind of full stop, like death, and like death
A 'point' is in the end a mystery,
Ambiguous and unknowable, yet
About which one might fabulate and/or
Contemplate and/or meditate until
The proverbial cows come home. And when
They do come, as they are linguistically
Required to do, they'll come to eat the grass
And frolic in their unremembered lives,
Unencumbered by memory or morals,
Chewing the cud their only concern. And that
My friends, is where the story ends. Full stop.

FREAK

And did you know I can see into you?
Your heart, your mind, your breath, yes, everything
Is visible to me like an x-ray
Machine or a TSA body scan,
But in place of the box-cutters, the guns,
The impotent unlit shoe-bomb, I see
Something else, the reason, or rather the
Reasoning out, the process by which each
Decision, however seemingly minor,
Gets made, how having just found yourself for
Instance standing on the sidewalk talking
To a friend, importuning him, no, wait,
That's too strong a word, "asking his advice"
About what to do next, because you see
A kind of mental fog had recently
Only recently in fact possibly
Even that very day lifted, maybe
'Had been' lifted, but if 'had been,' then by
What or by whom, what agent did the job,
What agency, not the TSA, who
As we know miss much, for instance, bodies
On the scanner screen glow white against black

~

While forbidden objects stand out against
The white, but as it turns out those objects
Stored at the margin of the body and
The black void disappear, allowing
Certain things to go unseen, the return
Of the repressed in the form of a weapon.
And so as I was saying the fog had
Recently lifted. I was standing on
A sidewalk with a friend who I had asked
To give me some advice. Just go, he said,
This city isn't going anywhere,
You can always come back, advice I took
Without much more of a thought. Fourteen years
Have passed, and I wonder if he is still
Standing there, on the sidewalk in New York,
Hearing the sound of his words leave his mouth
Watching some apparitional semblance
Of myself pause, feeling as I did
That everyone, including him, could see
His words as they entered my body, could
Watch them interact with every strand of
DNA, making ever-so-subtle
Adjustments to my make-up, could see
Not just the reasoning process but the

Non-reasoning one, the one I couldn't
See myself, wherein my mind was laid bare
Before all but me, and maybe I too
Am still there, pausing in that moment
Before the decision was made, the passive
Voice again, yes, it 'was' made, but by whom?
Where is the agent? Did this agency
Also lift the recently lifted fog?
Well, it wasn't really a fog so much
As a pall, a heavy ornamental
Cloth placed over a funeral casket,
In this case the casket belonged to my dad,
Having recently passed, why do they say
'Passed,' actually that's a pretty good word
Provided it's not followed by 'away,'
'Passed' works fine, as in 'passed by,' waved hello,
Smiled and drove off, and so my father,
A man who bought and sold and rented cars,
Had just passed, driven by whatever to
Some other whatever, some other place
Or state. A fog or pall had descended
On my mind, heavy, suffocating,
I needed a way out, a place to be,
Not wherever it was my father was

Driven off to. There I go again. Who
Was driving? That's really the question. Who
Was driving the motherfucking car?
Anyhow, I needed a place to go,
The great metropolis had suddenly grown
Too small to contain this grief, possibly
The whole world and anyhow I'd heard that
Buffalo had poetry. Poets and
Poetry. And that's what I was looking for,
Something to lift the fog or pall, which, now
That I think of it, had not been lifted,
No, not at all, it was temporary,
It followed me like that cloud in the poem,
I wander'd lonely as a cloud. Ever
Wonder about that apostrophe, why
Wordsworth removed the 'e'? It's because he
Had too many syllables, the numbers
Did not add up, and down came the knife,
Which wouldn't be necessary now, the
'-ed' having long since gone silent. I felt
Like that cloud without the daffodils to
Console me. Truth be told I could not
Have told you what a daffodil looked like.
They're blooming all over our yard just now,

I am happy to report, thanks to this
Freakish spring which might be evidence that
Global warming is here to stay. I mean,
Daffodils in Buffalo the 24th
Of March, who could've dreamed such a thing?

AS IF SOMEONE HAD READ HIS MIND

This is the poem that begins with a man
Who looks up from a book he's been reading
(It's *The Selected Poems of John Wieners*
To which he's returned for the umpteenth time
For inspiration) through the slatted blinds
To the empty street. Something he can feel
Has suddenly changed, there is an absence
Of pedestrians out walking their dogs,
Or cars parked on this or the other side,
Neighbors mowing lawns or pulling up weeds
From front yard garden beds, or that guy
Who sits on his stoop all summer, singing
The same three songs by Elton John, The Band,
And Van Morrison, in the same order.
I guess he hopes we like it (we do not).
Signs reading DO NOT STAND hang from trees
And light posts. They're coming to resurface
The street the next three days, we will be towed,
And maybe, he thinks, maybe what I feel
Is that, the expectation of something
About to arrive, the rumbling of trucks,
The acrid smell of burning tar, the mouths

Of the workers spewing obscenities
In jest or out of boredom or both.
I'm parked a ways away, on a cross street,
Whose only surviving sign is blank, sun
And rain and time having washed the words off,
Leaving behind another kind of
Anticipation, that of waiting for
A neon orange parking violation
Envelope to appear in the wiper.
I see the guy next door is offering
Parking spots in his backyard for ten bucks
And rain has been falling all day and I think
Perhaps this means they won't be paving
After all, that their work and our lack
Of parking will extend beyond Friday
Into the following week. It's now too late–
Even if sun did peek out–for the crews
To come. Work starts seven in the morning
Or it doesn't start at all. Union rules.
No matter, I return to Wieners' poem,
Engaged in taking away/from God his sound.

THE AUTHOR

Michael Kelleher is the director of the Windham-Campbell Literature Prizes at Yale University. He formerly served as Artistic and Associate Director of Just Buffalo Literary Center in Buffalo, New York, where he founded *Babel*, an international lecture series in which he interviewed authors such as V. S. Naipaul, Salman Rushdie and Zadie Smith.

His published collections of poetry include *Museum Hours* (BlazeVOX, 2016), *Human Scale* (BlazeVOX, 2007), and *To Be Sung* (BlazeVOX, 2004). His poems and essays have appeared in *The Brooklyn Rail*, *Colorado Review*, *The Poetry Foundation Website*, *Sentence: A Journal of Prose Poetics*, *ecopoetics*, *The Poetry Project Newsletter*, *EOAGH*, and others.

From 2008-13 he produced a blog project entitled "Aimless Reading," in which he documented the more than 1,200 books in his personal library.

CHAX

Chax was founded in 1984 in Tucson, Arizona. Located in the University of Houston-Vicctoria Center for the Arts in Victoria, Texas since 2014, Chax has published more than 200 books in a variety of formats, including hand-printed letterpress books and chapbooks, hybrid chapbooks, book arts editions, and trade paperback editions, such as the book you are holding that has been the recipient of generous support from UHV and many friends of the press. Chax is an independent 501(c)(3) organization that depends on support from various government and private funders and, primarily, from individual donors and readers.

You may find Chax online at *http://chax.org.*